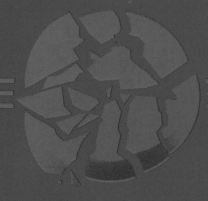

Dirty Talk

Listen, even a lullaby can bleed
                    —Osip Mandelstam

Say my name like the last bright syllable
of olive in a martini glass, your tongue

an eel deranged with moonlight
squiggling at the bottom of a gasoline-

dark sea. I've tested all the condoms,
filled them with champagne, imagined

a tiny house inside the reservoir tip
where unborn children catch fireflies in a wet field,

their fingers pulsing with light
every time we play Pull-Out Roulette

or the latex doesn't break, a choreography
of blackout and bioluminescence plagiarized

from an oyster's bristled sheen. Love, we are ancient
as the first people who learned to screw standing up

against a pine tree. Only your murmurs can staunch
the fissures inside me. Touch me like an assassin

strokes the steps of a church. Say my name
until I glow, engorged and radiant

as a tick boasting her blood-swollen
hunger without shame.
                    —Kendra DeColo

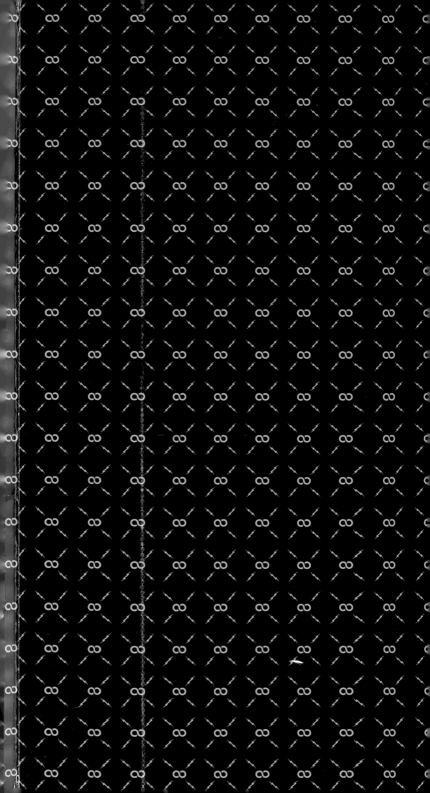

MY DINNER WITH
RON JEREMY

THIRD MAN BOOKS
NASHVILLE, TENNESSEE

Also by Kendra DeColo:

Thieves in the Afterlife (Saturnalia Books 2014)

MY DINNER WITH RON JEREMY

BY KENDRA DECOLO

Listen to Kendra DeColo:
http://thirdmanbooks.com/mydinnerwithronjeremy
password: GoldSoundz

Printed in Nashville, Tennessee

Library of Congress Control Number: 2016942602

FIRST EDITION
Design and Illustrations by Ryon Nishimori

ISBN   978-0-9913361-4-2

for AK and EMK

Come love let us sit together
In the cramped kitchen breathing kerosene.

-Osip Mandelstam

CONTENTS

The Perfect Aura

To have the confidence of a mannequin
stripped and starving on display

is half-way to being human as I am half-
way there most days, remembering

to be thankful for my teeth and good vision,
the taste of grapefruit and a woman's

full voice singing *fuck you*
as we pass briefly on the street,

the gift of invisibility granting me
another moment of freedom.

And then there are days when I envy
the plaster limbs poised in store windows,

anemic auras grafted from steel
and artificial starlight, the un-desperateness

to live that will outlast us. My sister
tells me her aura has its own dopplegänger,

smart as a radar looping around her inner-
self, her body shining like a car dealership.

She never worries someone will see
through the mesh of shaved metal, the red

halo of her wig. If I had her armor
I would wear it like my favorite station

leaking repeat hits from a boom box,
slow and dangerous as a summer

verging on mayhem, loud enough
to remind every person I pass

that we were once a choreography
of particles glittering in the same

discotheque's blackout, that says:
I am trying to transmit you

something, to reside in your ether,
not a confession but one long unfolding

salutation, like the sign at White Castle
whose message changes each Sunday

where I'm often stopped at a red light
wishing for someone's hand

to touch me at the clavicle, to leave
a stain deep enough to last.

They Said I'd Never Be a Dancer

even though I was born into the family
business—half-off Tuesdays at the Gilded

Cage—the club my uncle owned
and kind of place that paid

in beer and arcade coins, where women's
tasseled parts were out-glittered

by skee-ball prizes and slot machine
music. My ankles were too thick

to work the club so I performed
back-up moves at Bar Mitzvahs,

taught middle school boys how
to two-step and fake the Cotton-

Eyed Joe while their parents observed,
a naughty gleam in their eye, fisting

over the night's tip saying, "You girls
really worked it tonight," and I didn't

even break a sweat but once
got sentimental watching a girl

in braces get felt up for the first time,
imagining the ride home in her father's

minivan, murmuring into the cold
rolled-up windows when asked

about her night and all she remembers
is the sticky residue, the glimmer

of contraction in her chest,
how she'll never be good at math

again, concerned only with the shape
of her stunted breasts after hearing

her groping-partner the next day
tell a classmate that it felt like touching

skittles taped to a rock, and don't make me
tell you it builds character, don't make

me lie and say I intervened
as he shoved her against the tinseled

walls of Sammy's Roumanian
while the pitchers of chicken fat

gleamed and shivered on the table,
that I took her hand and said

"Darling, let's hoof it," and we danced
like lunatics until our ligaments shone.

Christian Camp for Troubled Girls

I liked to get felt up by the blonde
banker's daughter who wore overalls

and had a smoker's cough, who kept
a pet rat and folded Marlboro Reds

into the cuff of a white shirt in a way
that reminded me years later

of a man I loved in Spain with wide
shoulders and a slick ponytail

who broke a goalie's jaw after a soccer match
and we all drank beers together that same night,

pissing behind the jasmine bushes
on the hazy walk home. I've never known

how to act around a man throwing
a tantrum, weeping because his mother

was a prostitute and made him chocolate
sandwiches between jobs, how it still breaks

his heart to look at a tub of Nutella, or the fit
where something gets smashed, window

or plate. I tried it myself once during a fight
and it felt good to release the porcelain

face, hurl it against the wall to make a point.
We'd been arguing about his porn addiction

again, or maybe it was his stinginess,
how he accused me of watching videos

without chipping in, even though I covered
his rent. Maybe, I screamed, *I will not pay*

to watch a Brazilian woman get shit on,
as the dish flew from my glossy palm

like a dove out of a magician's hat.
Or I proclaimed, *I refuse*

to be shit on, and that's how I knew
it was time to get out. They taught us

at camp how to make lanyards and bridle
a horse, but all I want to remember is the ribbon

of sweat on my friend's upper lip,
how she let me win every time

we arm wrestled, how she made me feel strong
before she pinned me to the ground.

The Retired Contortionist Inside You

Sprawled atop the bed
of a truck where high school boys

suck tequila from your neck,
your body anonymous

as a lesser comet,
nipples smeared like emergency

flares, it takes three men
to fasten the jacket,

hold you while a needle
spits serum

into your blood
but I remember how we slept

feather boa and margarine-
hearted, evicted

from every karaoke bar
and dormitory, absinthe-

lit and rolling under bad
sound systems, the rash

of synthetic underwear
and static staining our skin.

I didn't know what was
waiting when I cupped

my ear to your ribs,
a constellation of sores

and glands rasping between us,
how I would be the one

you'd call, years later, your voice
dry and reaching through

the hospital payphone
asking for help, a retired

contortionist unfolding
inside you, waiting

to spill back into the world
like gasoline.

When You're 15 and the Hospital Pharmacist Hits on You While Filling Your Prescription for Plan B

Resist the urge to give him your phone number.
Tell him he looks good in white, because he does. Do not peel
back the gauze at the crease of your elbow. Do not look
at the small glint of blood, remembering
the first time a man pulled your tampon out with his teeth,
or the English teacher or the friend's father.
Tell the pharmacist, sorry, the phlebotomist already asked you out.
Tell him you said yes because he tapped your vein
like a fuse, humming to its fattest point, that he drew your blood
with a patience so inconsequential it hurt, and the white walls
stung while you waited together for the vials to fill,
dark and oxygenated. That afterwards you craved
a glass bottle of coke, winced when he took
the needle out of its socket. Tell him this and leave
the smooth jazz and the boxes of cough syrup and Tylenol
in the luminous rows, touching each one before you go.
When he winks, let it fizzle into ash. Tell him your blood
is so thick it would ravage his veins.

Cheers

Massachusetts' highest court ruled Wednesday that it is not illegal to secretly photograph underneath a person's clothing—a practice known as "upskirting."
                                    —CNN March 6, 2014

Because a suit on all fours angled
his camera up the black miniskirt

my sister wore when she slung
fries at the Ground Round

during high school, a few miles
outside Fenway, better known

as the Green Monster, or is that
what they call jealousy, I forget,

his pinstripes brushing the peanut-
covered floor, you know the kind

of place, shepherd's pie, burnt ends,
stout for the thick-necked getting off

from work, I can't go to a Red Sox
game without imagining her

writing specials on a board
in bright chalk, tired from partying

the night before, unaware
of the man who didn't tip

and wears a Brooks Brothers suit
slipping his lens up her skirt,

but before my sister
can call for help, he's peeled

out the door like a man
stealing a base, like two men

run after pissing on a homeless man's
fractured skull in Harvard Square

adrenaline pumping in their fat
veins as they escape into an alley,

and she keeps working, wipes
the spilt beer, hears cheering

from the stadium as she hauls
trash at the end of the night

and years later will tell me
it was almost funny

how he thought he was getting
away with something

when there was almost
nothing left to take.

Gold Soundz

For E.M.W.

I can't stop singing that Pavement song,
the one that sounds like an old lime green
Volvo and bottles of Old E, like autumn
in the suburbs where rich kids do bad things
to each other in their enormous empty houses
and are still friends the next day. The truth
is that most of us would be fine, except
the ones who weren't, the guy I dated
with the shaved head and rotten front tooth
who lived in the woods with two pitbulls,
Honey Bear and Jack, and punched a hole
in my bedroom wall before he disappeared.
Or the friend who stopped taking her lithium
after college and married a man who months later
stabbed her in the backseat of a car, left her
bleeding to death on the side of an unmarked road
and I think we used to sing this song sometimes
on our drive to Walden Pond where we'd swim
topless and yell at the lurkers, the man
who once pulled it out and we laughed
at his sad gesture, and it's her laughter
I'm hearing now, her head resting on my shoulder
on the drive home, eating an apple
that had rested between my legs.
She was the kind of friend who'd laugh
that the apple smelled like pussy
and eat it anyway.

Getting Dressed

Some days you wear
a dress made of ignition

& starlight, run-off
from highways

whose scars are dim
constellations on a starlet's

wrist. Some days the road
is the violet dress

you wore to the dance
where your date

bragged he made you
respectable. Still,

you showed your face
to third period

English, smelling like leftover
vodka & watermelon,

even when your teacher smirked
as you entered, trying

to sit quietly at your desk,
& later offered you

a ride home, lit
your cigarette with a red

Bic. Still, you wrote
letters to a future

self, your hair
a plastic bag

to breathe into
& every song

on the radio
didn't return you

to your body
but gave you space

to feel the roughness
of fabric against

your skin, a starting
point, one small

pleasure to break
back into your life.

To My First

I should warn you, every guitar has its ghosts . . .
                                        —Patrick Rosal

Slick of muscle
and reverb lifted
from a musky case—

black and white
as a plastic cow's hide,
udders strapped

with kegs, gold
foam spurting
into drunken mouths—

beneath my delusions
of James Brown
and Little Wing

I played you with neon
in my blood, phosphor
dousing your neck,

a junky's stammer
and scarlet twitch,
formaldehyde tongue

and red mohawk
of the boy whose girl
I stole, sweet sticky

kiss, ellipsis
and staggered noon
hunting down

the last tingle
of electric teeth
and gun metal ache,

playing you until
my fingers bled,
until my bones shone.

Ukulele

Fat canary running scales
in a rusted cage, you have the ego
of a Stratocaster, opera singer performing

"Purple Rain" on the subway. I call you
The Velveteen Habit because of the way
you suck heat from my fingers

as if to steal my identity, thumb swirl
like ghost organs inked inside fetal
ribs. Sometimes I play you just to hear

the silences, indigo oozing
out of each fret like an infusion,
listening to fissures

flap and squish their tinny gills.
I could take a hammer to feel
the wood bend, orchestrate

a damage that moans and warbles—
melted resin, warped-in sternum,
the pulse and starry ether

of your insides. But I need you
chapeled and lit, hoarding all our secrets
like a vaporous priest.

After *Ballad of Sexual Dependency*

Nan, I've been trying to seduce your voluptuous
shadow, linger in the wet coils

of sulfuric light, walls yellowed
as nicotine fingers, nail beds cracked & split,

wanted to sink my face into the sticky, damp
pages when I first found you in Tim's Used Books,

already 18, not even close to a virgin, but might
as well have been, your image blow-torching

something inside, a desire I kept stacked
cleanly as linens, trying to train my thighs

to be thin & deferential, until you barged
in with your warbling, anemic courage,

rotted cowboy boots & curls rusted
at the edge of a frame, straddling a man

with ribs like a lead-chipped radiator. You were
better than Courtney Love, better than the girl

I let sleep in my bed with her combat boots
on, who left bruises on my neck and returned

to her rich parents' home the next day—
the real stitch of steel vein

I was searching for when I dragged a nail
half-heartedly across my arm, the salt & glass

in my throat when I drank a wino's stash
buried under a pier, dizziness & stink

lifting me into another octave
where I could disappear into the low tide haze.

Tell me it's not something we grow
out of. Tell me we can heal & keep our demons

trained, collared & fat inside of us.
That we can teach them to growl & sing

while happiness smolders at the edge
of a horizon we never thought to look for.

Interstate Pastoral

I don't trust what doesn't leave behind a shimmered
stain. For instance, the woman who uncrosses her legs
at the rest stop, flashing a tiny American flag—she must wax

for sure, I think. You can always tell by looking
at a person's clothes: dry-cleaned and ironed, smelling
like holy water mixed with Febreze. I wonder

if the gas station attendant knows I'm not the trimmest
bush on the block, that I tend to let the days
stack up to see how fast the wilderness sprawls, like kudzu

fingering a tree in the underpass, public showers
filled with pubic coils tangled in the drain's moonlit teeth,
the stacks of urinal cakes waiting to be placed

like sacraments into porcelain white mouths,
whispering, *imagine the things we've seen*
as they swirl, surrendering their neon, soporific hearts.

Marriage Tips

Don't fall in love with the fertility specialist
because she can chart the speed

at which your pupils dilate
when exposed to pleasure, hands

latexed and agile as she explains
why one's vibrator is vital to good health,

leaving purple marks to demonstrate
where the baby might be.

Don't masturbate in the same room
unless it's agreed upon, in which case

orchestrate good lighting and set the sound
machine to 'Rain Forest.' Let your moans

be the wet air rubbing against the banana
leaves. Kiss until you bruise

each others' mouths, seared as planetary
rings. Make-out like you're trying

to soak the leather seats of a Cadillac,
bodies crammed together as if to seal

the mouth of desire always whispering
more more more. When you hold hands,

pretend you've robbed a record store,
a million notes smoldering between your legs.

Listening to Coltrane's "In a Sentimental Mood"

Needle pricks of moonlight raked along a street's collapsed vein
The fire's other occupation
Orion swooning above a flame's blue skirt

Velvet upholstery drenched in a theater's back row seat
Green dress wrecked with cum
Bright morning I stagger into scattering dust of imploded cists

Scorched wings of a deranged saint
Missing teeth that make a prayer
Knife I use to cut notes bright as amphetamines

My fingers stunned from stroking an angel's bruised face
Coins from fountains gathered to swallow their evanescence
Rebirth and backwash of amniotic light

Silk of grief unraveling like an umbilical chord
Need for one yellow leaf that keeps spilling out of me
Cervix gilded as Grand Central's map of stars.

The Lovers on the Bridge (1991)

The sun like a nasal drip
setting over the Nashville skyline
makes me want to be a better lover, unclean

as Denis Lavant's bandaged
hand drawing *pyrotechnics like brainfire
in the brow*, penetrating a statue's

cracked silhouette, the way I once
crouched behind my high school
and pulled out a tampon

to leave something of myself
behind, engorged
as a blossom splaying its septic

heart. Imagine what it's like
to be seen so clearly you can't stop
seeing yourself, even when eyes

congeal into a milky residue
of corroded vessels burning
like the night sky, little stars

in the grooves a thumbtack
once made along the inner wrist.
That's how it was, pulling

myself out of my ex's arms
as he nodded off, a bare bulb
catching the calligraphy of necrotic

veins. I thought, this is what it means
to be in love, staggered and begging
a tab of acid from under my tongue,

the Buenos Aires sky smeared
like a face of Vaseline,
not the way Lavant's infected feet

keep the city whole, explosive
as dynamite in the belly of a fish,
but wanting to watch someone

incandesce, so full of what they love,
Binoche's bruised retinas
siphoning anodyne from the clamor

of her lover's bones, slamming together
like the city's last utterance, like *a death*
sentence that must be sung.

Church of OCD

Because someone has to do it
I count forgettable things:

yellow houses, birch trees
shaped like crooked priests,

the stitches on a porn star's shiny
lids. I watch Redtube and count

the number of times a woman
shouts "holy" while having

her hair braided by two men
dribbling whiskey into her mouth.

But there are things I want to know,
like at this moment, how many of us

are squeezing our left breast
with one hand while the other

traces a crack up the wall
that splits into deeper cracks.

The average number of days
before bread will break open

its green veins, gangrene blossoming
at the heel. How many people have

masturbated on carnival rides
watching a radio tower sparkle

in the distance, hands fluorescing
with secretions like the tiniest, lucky star.

Dirty Talk

Listen: even a lullaby can bleed.
                    —Osip Mandelstam

Say my name like the last bright syllable
of olive in a martini glass, your tongue

an eel deranged with moonlight
squiggling at the bottom of a gasoline-

dark sea. I've tested all the condoms,
filled them with champagne, imagined

a tiny house inside the reservoir tip
where unborn children catch fireflies in a wet field,

their fingers pulsing with light
every time we play Pull-Out Roulette

or the latex doesn't break, a choreography
of blackout and bioluminescence plagiarized

from an oyster's bristled sheen. Love, we are ancient
as the first people who learned to screw standing up

against a pine tree. Only your murmurs can staunch
the fissures inside me. Touch me like an assassin

strokes the steps of a church. Say my name
until I glow, engorged and radiant

as a tick boasting her blood-swollen
hunger without shame.

Self-Portrait with the Virgin Mary and Magic Mike

I didn't mean to forget myself in the theater
when I grabbed the stranger's hand

and pressed it to my half-swollen breasts
gushing with hormones, clamping

down as they struggled to break free.
I'm going to be a mother so I must be

responsible, I tell myself twenty times a day,
but can't stop wanting to walk past

the drive-thru window dressed in tassels,
demanding to be handfed bits of masticated bun,

skirt fanning open like a pigeon in heat. I can't
sit in a theater without wanting to ask

Channing Tatum out loud, *do you see us,*
do you love us the way we love you, my body

tingling like a tub of popcorn grease
with a hole cut out in the bottom.

When the Virgin Mary waited for Jesus
to be born, I don't imagine she prayed

to feel so much at once her body stumbled
inside itself like a drunk at a state fair

but maybe she understood pleasure
is a kind of knowing. Maybe she felt

so full with the world she stayed perfectly
still, dizzy with the sting of restraint.

Self-Portrait as a Country Song

Every town needs a woman
with bottle cap teeth

who can crack a cold one
between her legs, letting the froth

spill out like low tide
at Virginia Beach, who doesn't

give a shit she's too old
for the musicians

sipping Allagash
at the Red Door Saloon

and cackles *I play the twat*
before hitching up her skirt

and twiddling the wet stretch
of cotton like limp strings

of a miniature guitar,
who sneers, *how'd you like*

the show, teetering off
into the late afternoon sun

to watch her daughter
walk home from school,

pulsing with the kind
of thick, viscous love

I can't bear to imagine
my mother felt for me,

the way I once watched
an addict feed her blonde daughter

french fries at Wendy's before
nodding off in the back of their car

but for that moment they were
the two happiest people

I'd ever seen. I want to know
how the girl felt, draping

a sweater over her mother's
shuddering, thin frame,

if she kept watch, or drifted
off into her own world

the way I learned to stop feeling,
leaning against a radiator

to siphon rusted music
between my legs.

But every town needs
a mother who makes a light show

of her grief, spinning around
the supermarket,

warbling at the top of her lungs
you are my sunshine,

who knows what it's like
to play the town fool,

guarding our sadness
like a locket under her tongue,

spilling its light when she cracks
open its rusty jaws to sing.

Break-Up Letter to My Clitoris

Just because we don't hang out
anymore doesn't mean

you aren't the single synthetic jewel
affixed to a dancer's umbilicus,

last coin thumbed into a slot
machine's decadent gleam.

To be a gargoyle above your
baroque foyer is more magnificent

than a water birth in the Playboy
Mansion, more opulent

than finding free condoms
in the back of a limousine

but when I rise from the climate-
controlled leather seats

and leave behind a sleek stain,
it is a desolation. To think, one day

my fluids will take on a different
hue, and I will move through the world

dry as a penny. But you, clitoris,
will be entitled to every susurrus

of joy, a jukebox with one tiny
record looping inside.

We Are All Made of Stars

All this backwash and fizzle,
all this sucked-up helium and dirty talk

like perverted saints. Face it, the failed
orgy is over. The freeloaders

have gone home to stroke themselves
in the dank privacy of their dens

lit by the soft murmur of a desktop.
Ron Jeremy, where were you

when we needed you, patron saint
of the horny who still like to crack

a few wise ones, who go to temple
on the high holidays and enjoy

sharing their spouse? When did it get
so hard to peg your neighbor while looking

each other in the eye? Ron Jeremy,
you don't even own a cell phone.

You're a relic, selling boutique
vodka called The Silver Schmeckle,

a living bobblehead whose penis
wobbles like an obelisk

ribbed with halos and discontinued
condoms. Still, I like to think

we're all in this together
when we close the door, entering

uncharted space as you don
an astronaut's suit made of foil.

And when you mount the alien with four
breasts, we remember how vast

our own desires, how beautiful
to make love in another dimension

where we know we're not alone,
where our holes are filled with stars.

Interlude: Ron Jeremy Film or Kid's Show We Watched in the '80s?

1. I Was a Teenage Werebear
2. Detention
3. Gerald McBoing Boing
4. Tetherball: The Movie
5. Pizza
6. Simply Stephanie
7. Eight is Enough
8. Fist of the North Star
9. In Your Face
10. Little Red Riding Hood
11. 3-2-1 Contact
12. Pole Position
13. Relax, He's My Stepdad
14. Squirt Wars
15. Hello Kitty's Furry Tale Theater
16. Beverly Hills Teens
17. The Crack Pack
18. Highway to Heaven
19. The Pearl Divers
20. Crazy Animal
21. The Secret Life of Toys

Ron Jeremy Films: 1, 2, 4, 5, 6, 9, 10, 13, 17, 19, 20

Kid's Shows I watched in the '80s: 3, 7, 8, 11, 12, 15, 16, 18, 21

Neither: 14

Prelude to an Attempt at Autoerotic Asphyxiation

Arbitrary, the array of sanitized riggings,
smooth jazz in the background

like a processional for when I come
back to my body, ravenous

for salt, returning from the fluency
of vapor, tremoloed medusas

swishing in the estuary of my pores.
I've never been good at precision

but can fake a high note
when singing along with Prince,

can make myself dizzy
posing perfectly still—the secret

to pleasure, I think: the point
before you become sick

with yourself, the room full of
rancid auras, starless jellies

writhing in their sleeves, how a woman
once pressed down on my chest

after I breathed into the tent
of my hands, called it *Space Monkeys*,

and maybe this is what I'm after,
not disintegration but the pressure

of her palm, some force to be
reckoned with, to reduce me to light.

Watching Stepdad Porn

Watching stepdad porn
is like sleeping with the news on,

sticky with fog and last night's
tragedy drizzled over my blacked-out

body, Anderson Cooper's
voice etched into every orifice.

It's like imagining how it feels
to be a man's daughter, loved

the wrong way, touched
without tenderness, my mother

picking me up from school
with a herpes outbreak

on her face, gummy with pus
and antiviral cream,

nerves scrawled into flames
across her chin, thrilling

as the throb of an orange alert,
like wanting to be plugged

with fraudulent ballots, parade
peacock-feathered passed closed-down

voting halls in districts where the South
moans, arching backwards

like a finger-trap,
like news networks

re-playing the same bootlegged
footage, even though we've seen

the "cream pie" ending
which is really just a double facial—

endured the bad dialogue
and waited for the money

shot that never comes,
on our knees trying to rub-out

some belief in the numb
blue light.

Donald Trump Rides the Escalator of My Erotic Dreams

There are days when all I have is the slickness
of marigolds in the overturned gazebo of my chest,

greasy sparrows squabbling over Vicodin crumbs,
wanting something to hold my body

together like the tongues of pundits
who divide the hours between primetime

and dusk, loose minutes dissolved in the juices
of monogamous fucking. I went to a sex addicts' meeting

to get laid but only found men who like to watch
water stains march across hotel ceilings like animal

crackers in a wasted circus. It wasn't loneliness
that drove me to vote against my own interests

but something like it, how a friend who doesn't
want you still offers to hold you in their arms

until you feel sedate, swaddled in medicinal
pantyhose, diabetic socks, and you could drift

into a sea of serotonin, soft-shoed and dribbling
like a broken teleprompter, *I need I need I need.*

But Donald, I've never liked it gentle,
prefer it raw like my first time: face down,

no jelly. You don't need to look
me in the eye. Just give me enough heat

to forget who I am, your arms two electric eels
squiggling around the hull of my veiny, patriot heart.

Fantasy

Like a perv in a pickle park,
do you ever feel you're standing outside

your own life, raccoon-fisting
through trash, heavy-

breathing thick orchards
of fog across windshields,

watching the scenes unfold
like a montage of favorite

Bang Bus episodes, highlight
reels of bukaki-reverence,

open-sore epiphanies
and the inevitable spermicidal

come-down? I used to follow
nice cars on highways, get off

at their exit, split
before the roads turned

residential but one time I made it
to a small town's enormous

synagogue and, true story,
the driver of the silver Audi

was Ron Jeremy.
It was a High Holiday

and the street was loaded
with bright leaves. I waited

all night for him to come
out, imagining how good

it would feel: the two of us
at a diner eating soft-boiled

eggs, talking about the last
time we felt truly seen.

His green eyes would sputter
with gratitude and recognition—

how two shmucks like us
got to be so lucky

I don't know, he'd say
taking a long sip—

But he didn't see me
buckled-in and waiting

and besides, I'm not built
for that kind of pleasure.

Food for the Apocalypse

Hot Dog, I salute your compact elegance,
Slim Jim silhouette gristled and soaked

with nitrates, sodium lung like the cylindrical
heart of a lantern, flaring your negligee

of amphetamines. I will eat you to mark another
day on this earth, at a gas station in Indiana

where the tub of relish is phosphorus,
almost hallucinogenic as the innards

of a lava lamp, smashed and mixed
with bong water. I will be generous, too,

with the mustard whose glow-in-the-dark
moniker reminds me of the first scribble

of ejaculation in my palm at the movies
where we ate hot dogs during the previews,

my hand salty and damp with grease—
but I will be sparing with the ketchup,

used only out of nostalgia and respect
for its indestructability, a food that can

be compared to nothing else, possessing
its own logic of taste, ethereal

and bodily, what we will eat when the world
gives its last shudder and we search the burnt

husks of Kum & Go's for those pearlescent
packs, crenellated edges to be torn into

with our teeth. It will fill us with faith
in our impermanence, remind us

of a time when we ate out of our hands
for pleasure and watched images flash

across screens, some of us suffering, some
dragged across a classroom by a police officer

whose flesh was not unlike our own, kin
to this government-sanctioned meat.

Cocktail Hour at the Petting Zoo

I want to go to cocktail hour
        at the petting zoo

where the fainting goats blackout
        on fainting couches

and miniature sheep rest their haunches
        on pillows made of human hair—

I want to feed beer nuts and ambrosia
        salad to the parrot who plucks

feathers from her grey chest
        and sings "My Baby

Just Cares for Me," punctuated
        by a busted smoker's hack.

I'd buy her an Old Fashioned
        and listen to stories

about the woman who kept her locked
        inside a tapestry

covered cage, taking her out
        at night to teach her how

to sing, and I'd tell her about the man
        who'd slip postage stamps

of acid under my tongue while I slept,
        waking to our room

needled with fire, the roots
        of my teeth extinguished stars,

repeating the story until I realize
        I'm drunk and take one

for the road—not before stroking the muzzle
        of Clementine, the cow who lived

strapped to milk machines for years,
        surrendered one calf after the other,

and now likes to stay perfectly still
       in her green velvet corner,

nuzzling the flowered astroturf
       as if she has all the room she needs.

Playlist for a Strip Tease

Sometimes while driving,
the windshield smeared

with late afternoon light,
I remember my body,

how it shook involuntarily
the way rain convulses

above a parking lot
whenever I was touched.

My sister chooses
songs, not for their rhythm

but emotion, hands palming
asterisks to her back,

dancing as if underwater
to music that makes

men feel less finite as they
watch her translate words

into gesture, legs lacquered
under black lights, mimicking

opiate and bruised mouths.
There isn't a place I've slept

without carving her initials,
sometimes confusing

the syllables of our name.
What I mean to say is

every wreckage keeps something
of the body, particles boosted

from a dream, the white hatchback
in another city guarding gristle

of my twenty-year old skin,
plastered and begging

for a blackout, to be anonymous
as a body numinous

and drenched in blue light,
dancing slow enough

to dissolve, to become
beautiful again.

There Are Things I Won't Tell My Daughter

The lover who pierced his scrotum
with a cube of ice and screw

sterilized in a Bic's small flame,
how he said it felt like a tiny bell

ringing in the church of his body.
Or the girlfriend who drew spirals

of blood when she thrashed inside me,
amniotic pink and trickling down

my thighs like a watercolor.
I won't tell her about the smell

of vomit on a staircase in Madrid
where I used my body to secure

a place to sleep. The banker who spat
into me like a well. The taste of cold eggs

the next morning, mouthwash and windex
to wash my cervix clean. I won't tell her

either, stories my mother told me,
the stranger who watched her fold

clothes at the laundromat while I
twitched in her belly, how he scribbled

the glass with murky cum. I won't tell her
the wreckage and blossom of red light filling

a parked car. Why I never reported it.
How I learned to stay in my body

long enough to feel the bloom
and thud of my heart that is a shack

of honeysuckle and shot of grease.
That is a trail of staggered stars

a needle left along my inner arm.
I will tell her about the color of fire escapes

in the city where she was conceived,
the bowl of oranges in the kitchen,

my body a fortune, a record,
a lamp post in the dusk.

How snow covered us all winter
and I walked outside, happy

and delirious, collecting the blue
shards on my tongue.

Low-End Theory

Love, I'm a musky vermouth, palm of discount
stars, instruction manual for low-end vibrators

which is to say, my frequencies have slowed
down to the flutter of a junebug's libido,

slow but steady, now that I'm with child
and cast my desires across the earth

like a plastic lure. I think the earth is obscene
sometimes, its jeweled ligaments and glands

bedazzled with poisons, designed to seduce
us into curated oblivions. I've been sober

five years and still don't know what to do
with all this beauty, my serotonin receivers

cracked and humming. Even the news
playing on a deli's small TV set is a pleasure

I will one day miss, how the blonde host's
lips are opulent as bloodworms at low tide

shimmying under a full moon, and the footage
of protesters looks like believers frothing

to be sedated with holy touch, even the one
who carries a sign that says "If we killed fetuses

with guns, would the liberals care then?"
But I still can't help thinking that someone

made this sign with their own hand,
that it's possible to love an idea until

you forget what love means, and doesn't
this light show of vitriol remind me

that I, too, am dissolving back into the earth,
that we are just pre-ejaculate glittering

on god's ornate tip that will keep spurting
long after we're gone? Let me love

even this anchor asking, *don't all lives
matter.* Let this love be enough

to keep me going, trudging through
a spectacle that shimmers like shit

flecked with gold, a rancid honey
whose sweetness obliterates as it shines.

Palmistry

It took me a long time to stop letting strangers
read my palm. They'd grab my hand on the subway

or in basement cafés, running a cold finger along
the galactic crease shooting up toward the auroras

of my knuckles, a silver nerve twinkling like a straw
in a glass of vodka. They'd whisper wetly into my ear

things like: "You drink too much" and "Be careful
who you trust." It became a sticky kind of addiction, swirling

concussion as the future unspooled from a mystic's
jaundiced tongue. I stayed away from the professionals though—

didn't trust their animated divinations, hamming it up
like a church organist's fist concocting revelation.

But one woman, the clairvoyant who ran a moving
company and sat next to me at the McDonald's

café, named the exact day that I would meet you—
said it over her shoulder like an afterthought

as she tossed a plastic cup of iced coffee into the trash
and that was all I needed to hear, to be ready and waiting

at the right moment, under the magnolia, where our two
paths converged, where you kissed my empty palm.

Sometimes God's Work is Sloppy but it's Always on Time

Today I watched a crow with too much
time on its hands steal feathers

from a hawk's golden haunches,
just for the hell of it, stalking

suburban streets whose trees
soak up aspirations from vision

boards of college students, roots
nourished by dregs of unfinished

dreams. The thick bark reminds me
of Dr. Phil's hands, groping our

subconscious like a smooth tollbooth
operator, the back of his bald head

shiny as a lit-up map where you can
find every recorded act

of human decency
and I don't mean to brag

but I once spent the day
watching over a tuft of tilled earth

where a turtle had laid her eggs,
right in the middle of a busy walkway.

Maybe she was distracted or had a lot
on her plate, but goddamnit,

she got the job done, squeezing
out each leathery wet egg.

After she scuttled off
into the marsh behind a Wendy's

I stood watch over the fresh mound
and sang to the embryos, brand new

in their woozy shells. I procured
some chalk and drew a pink heart

around the site, writing
in big letters: Caution,

Fragile Life Here—
which is what I say to strangers

when my aura gets dim
and I need an extra layer

of protection to steady me
through the days' unraveling reels

of atrocities. I'll point
to my chest and remember

how joy survives,
humming through the cracks

of accidental grace,
making a home out of nothing.

I Can't Stop Thinking About the Room

where Coltrane wrote A *Love Supreme*,
        the second floor carpet

plush and piled as a priest's
        robe, the color of a roller rink

at midnight when the slow song
        grinds through speakers

and glossy orbs scatter fish-scales
        of light across the smooth floor,

lovers sweating into each others'
        fists, scissoring their skates

while the arcade machines and tanks
        of neon prizes crackle

and hum, plugged like umbilical chords
        into the deep sockets—

I can't stop thinking of the ointment
        sheen, lava lamp ovum

pulsing against the cathedral
        of highway sounds

where he wrestled with his angels,
        smeared with ink and ash,

an indigo, almost violent
        shade of purple, smoldering

like a lounge player's tuxedo,
        the asterisked mouths

of cigarette burns dim and constellated,
        Draco dragging his stalactite

tail over some half-dead sea—
        cough syrup glow, spoon

held to a bare bulb. If auras exist,
        this is what I choose:

liquor store candescence
            of a confessional booth,

a street wet with voices
            where I walk, holding the swell

of narcotics transmuted
            into testament, holy

itch and resonance
            of footsteps pressed

into the shag, this purple life,
            making a road out of prayer.

Instrumentation: Conception

Give me a piano key, a whistle,
              any instrument to match

this miniscule spark, cusping
              rusted areolas

of a saxophone, stubbing my tongue
              to summon one clear note.

I want to thread my fingers
              through the morning's

filaments like a glass harp,
              loamy echo casting its lush

lure across the city
              as this new life hums

inside me, an orchestration
              I already know but can't

play, not yet as we stumble through
              this borough whose rose-

colored stoops garnished with wet
              plastic blossoms, advertisements

for tune-ups and delivery, have become
              our temporary home

where each morning I bring us
              bagels and cream cheese,

improvising my body
              through this new winter light.

Quickening

Sticky as a film of blue pollen on a windshield,
flash of half-notes, clustered aphids jeweling a leaf,

your movement is microscopic, breakbeat
and blossom, language of brine shrimp and half-

opened shells pulling syllables from the moon's
alkaline throat. You are more memory

than dream, the fog I wake into, cloudy
as the thawed water of street geraniums

pulsing in a white bucket, bright sting
I want to put my lips to and drink

when you buckle like a star, as I want to keep
everything beautiful intact when my insides

start to tingle with this midnight code, go back
and lift the bird I once found into its nest,

return music and blood and reverb to the body
before it knew how to feel, to be brave enough

to claim this small joy, your silk and drizzle
synchronizing with the thrum of my lopsided heart.

Apricots

Sleek as a doorknob in July, you turn
inside me even though I can't yet feel
your movements, the size of a silver
dollar, dried apricot, the fruit I will eat

when your tongue spurs like an invocation
and you taste what smolders in my palm:
spoons of honey, sting of air
when I wake up early to see

the road still wet from last night's
rain. It is leathery and scrotal
and not my favorite fruit but makes me
think of the word *mish mish*,

what your grandmother called
the gift she'd smuggle into prison
when visiting her son, wax paper bags
filled with pistachios and bright

orange discs, stitched into the seam
of her dress, how she rode the bus
from New York to Pennsylvania
each week and piled them

into his hands, a dome of contraband
light that I can still feel pulsing
like a last kiss, the taste of tough
skin that once broke in a hungry mouth.

Coming Home

I've got hostess crumbs on my shirt,
fresh scorch marks on my thighs,

calico scars from gas station coffee
spilled while listening to news

on NPR, the smell of skin
ruptured and pocked, pain mingled

with stories of Syria, Benghazi,
the toxic-flag of Donald Trump's

hair. I've got old matchbooks
and ticket stubs in my pocket, a fist

of sticky cassette tapes from yard sales—
Bobby 'Blue' Bland's *Greatest Hits*

listened to 20 times
on the drive from New York

to Nashville when my radio
broke, the morphine drip

of tremolo and twang rippling
through me like summer light

the year I stopped drinking
where the chords and hot air whipped

back and forth through the open
window, loving me wet and sloppily

as he sang out each letter
of his name. I've got no change

for the tollbooth and a glove
compartment full of expired

condoms, but I have the resin
of his voice in my lungs,

the ghost of a song played
until the ribbon disintegrates,

looped around me like a halo,
spelling out my new name.

Interstate Pastoral

Today I want to praise the lewd radiance
of a neighbor's grass, shellacked pesticide-green,

the glossalalia of sparrows ransacking a split-open
sack of fries in the underpass where someone

scrawled *Jesus Saves*, the glyphs striated,
seeping down toward the half-finished handle

of whiskey, which makes a kind of hush
I could dissolve inside of, erratic scripture

of tire marks and entrails, someone's lips
that warmed the glass leaving a permanent kiss.

I once preferred to be anonymous, translucent
and tinged with the essence of being a person

like the Heirloom Asparagus Water at Whole Foods
that people buy for nine dollars so they can forgive

being in their bodies a little longer,
like paying to watch women stick cucumbers

into each others' assholes to disguise
the feeling of being alone, ghostly as the lawn mower's

engine sending a rusted orgasm against
the late autumn ambience,

how every passing car reminds me of waking
to a stranger's cold hands, rearranging

my insides. If I'm whole, it's because
I fought to be here, stepping into clean underwear

that is summer blue with tiny hearts, bought
out of the hard-fisted belief that I might feel

joy again, not stumbling inside the vertigo
of desire but facing the day with a beautiful

terror, tying my laces or washing my face
with a tenderness that wrecks me.

Sober at the Waffle House

I want to be where the syrup jars glint
like lanterns, diaphanous and tinted
as the amber glaze of a parked Chevy's
windshield on a Friday night. I'll sit at the counter
and listen to the short order cook argue
with the waitress about proper ways
to please a woman, sipping from thick-rimmed
cups of weak coffee, wondering if anyone knows
where I am, 2 a.m. at this rest stop, deep
in rural Kentucky, near the Holiday Inn
where I won't spend the night, but will finish
my coffee and watch a feral cat stalk
a wounded sparrow in the parking lot,
wings fluttering like fake lashes
of a woman knocking back cheap
champagne, trying to remember the last time
she pursued anything with equal parts curiosity
and hunger. Or was it cruelty. Or was it delight.

NOTES

The collection's epigraph is taken from Osip Mandelstam's poem, "Night Piece," translated by Christian Wiman.

The epigraph of "To My First" is taken from Patrick Rosal's poem, "Guitar."

"*The Lovers on the Bridge* (1991)" was written after Leos Carax's film, *Les Amants du Pont-Neuf*, starring Juliette Binoche and Denis Lavant. The italicized lines are taken from Osip Mandelstam's poem, "Memories of Andrey Bely."

The epigraph of "Dirty Talk" is taken from Osip Mandelstam's poem, "Flat," translated by Christian Wiman.

"We Are All Made of Stars" takes its title from the Moby song whose music video features a cameo by Ron Jeremy.

"Prelude to an Attempt at Autoerotic Asphyxiation": Space Monkeys is a game in which one forces themselves to hyperventilate and another person hits them in the chest, causing a blackout.

"Food for the Apocalypse" references the 2015 incident in Richland Country, South Carolina where a police officer assaulted a black female high school student, body-slamming and dragging her across the classroom floor.

"Low-End Theory" takes its title from A Tribe Called Quest's second album of the same name.

"I Can't Stop Thinking About the Room" was inspired by the essay, "The Coltrane Home in Dix Hills" by Andy Battaglia, published in *The Paris Review* online. The title was inspired by Diane Seuss' poem, "I can't stop thinking of that New York skirt, turquoise sequins glued onto sea-colored cotton."

"Quickening" is the term for early fetal movements felt in utero.

"Apricots": Mish mish is the Arabic word for apricots. It is also part of the Arabic expression: "Bukra fil mish-mish" which can be translated as "tomorrow there will be apricots."

"Coming Home" refers to the Bobby 'Blue' Bland song, "Little Boy Blue."

ACKNOWLEDGEMENTS

Thank you to the editors and journals where these poems were first published, at times in earlier versions:

Copper Nickel	"The Retired Contortionist Inside You"
Cream City Review	"Palmistry" and "Prelude to an Attempt at Autoerotic Asphyxiation"
Gulf Coast Online	"Low-End Theory"
Indiana Review	"Getting Dressed" and "The Perfect Aura"
Nashville Review	"Dirty Talk" and "Sometimes God's Work is Sloppy but it's Always on Time"
Ninth Letter	"Donald Trump Rides the Escalator of My Erotic Dreams," "Self-Portrait with the Virgin Mary and Magic Mike," and "There Are Things I Won't Tell My Daughter"
Poetry Northwest	"I Can't Stop Thinking About the Room" and "Interstate Pastoral"
The Journal	"Christian Camp for Troubled Girls"
Tupelo Quarterly	"Playlist for a Strip Tease"

First and foremost, thank you to the incredible team at Third Man Books. Chet Weise and Ben Swank, thank you for your vision and belief in this manuscript. This book wouldn't have come into being without you. Thank you, Ryon Nishimori, for the gorgeous cover art and illustrations. Chet, thank you for being the best and most badass editor a poet could hope for. You make the poetry world a more generous and inspiring place.

Endless gratitude to the MacDowell Colony where most of these poems were written and where I was taken such good care of during my pregnancy.

Love and gratitude to the following people who read and supported these poems in their earliest stages: Tiana Clark, Katie

Greene, Allison Inman, Jennifer Leonard, Keith Leonard, Jeffrey McDaniel, Tyler Mills, Margaret Roarke, Lindsey Rome, Ciona Rouse, and Elizabeth Townsend.

Thank you Keetje Kuipers, Adrian Matejka, and Patrick Rosal for your kind words and for being my poetry heroes.

Thank you to the Korine family for your love and support (especially Rachel and Harmony for the story that inspired some of these poems).

To my family, always, for teaching me love and decency.

To Elia—you were part of me as I wrote these words. And to Avi—every poem in this book is for you.